THREE DEGREES OF
GLORY

THREE DEGREES OF
GLORY

Joseph Smith's Insights on the Kingdoms of Heaven

LAWRENCE R. FLAKE

Covenant Communications, Inc.

Covenant®

Cover drawing *School of the Prophets* © Liz Lemon Swindle, Repartee & Foundation Arts

Cover design copyrighted 2000 by Covenant Communications, Inc.

Published by Covenant Communications, Inc.
American Fork, Utah

Printed in the United States of America
First Printing: August 2000

07 06 05 04 03 02 01 00   10 9 8 7 6 5 4 3 2

ISBN 1-57734-698-X

ACKNOWLEDGEMENTS

I express my sincere appreciation to my friend and exemplar, Elder Vaughn J. Featherstone of the First Quorum of the Seventy, for his encouragement in making the Prophet's remarkable poem more accessible to members of the Church. I am thankful to a number of my admirable colleagues in Religious Education at Brigham Young University for reading the manuscript: Dean Robert L. Millet, Drs. Leon R. Harshorn, Joseph Fielding McConkie, Stephen E. Robinson, and Richard N. Holzapfel. I am also grateful to the Church Historical Department and Dr. Kent Jackson for the photographs and the facsimile of the poem. I am especially indebted to my wife, Elaine, for her valuable assistance in preparing the manuscript.

TABLE OF CONTENTS

INTRODUCTION

Most Latter-day Saints are familiar with the marvelous revelation concerning the kingdoms of glory recorded in section 76 of the Doctrine and Covenants, but relatively few have heard of Joseph Smith's remarkable poetic rewriting of this revelation. This glorious manifestation, recounted in both scripture and poem, was received simultaneously by the Prophet Joseph Smith and Sidney Rigdon on February 16, 1832. It was given as a series of six visions that together lasted over one hour. This heavenly outpouring so impressed the early Saints that they came to refer to it simply as "The Vision." President Wilford Woodruff placed it in a class by itself among all revelations:

> When I read these solemn, these eternal declarations made through the mouth of Joseph Smith, my heart swells with gratitude and praise to God, my heavenly Father. I consider that the Doctrine and Covenants, our Testament, contains a code of the most solemn, the most Godlike proclamations ever made to the human family. I will refer to the "Vision" alone, as *a revelation which gives more light, more truth, and more principle than any revelation contained in any other book we ever read (Journal of Discourses,* 22:146–147; italics added).

Elder Melvin J. Ballard called the Vision "The greatest revelation the Lord, Jesus Christ, has ever given to man, so far as record is made, . . . the climax of all wonderful revelations that have come from the Lord from the days of Father Adam until the present moment" ("Three Degrees of Glory," Salt Lake City: Magazine Printing Company, 1955).

The day the Vision was received, the prophet Joseph Smith wrote down his feelings about it:

> That document is a transcript from the record of the eternal world. The sublimity of the ideas; the purity of the language; the scope for action; the continued duration for completion, in order that the heirs of salvation may confess the Lord and bow the knee; the rewards for faithfulness, and the punishments for sins, are so much beyond the narrow-mindedness of men, that every honest man is constrained to exclaim: *"It came from God"* (*History of the Church*, 1:252–253).

Eleven years later, just eighteen months before his death, the Prophet wrote his poetic version of the Vision. This short book will acquaint Latter-day Saints with Joseph's literary and spiritual gem entitled "The Answer: A Vision," and point out some insights taken from its stanzas. Because the poem is largely a paraphrase of Doctrine and Covenants section 76, readers should not expect to find many profound new truths in it. Rather, they will discover insights and clarifications that illuminate and amplify the scriptural text. The importance of the poem is not that it breaks new doctrinal ground, but that it brings additional light to help us better understand one of the greatest revelations ever recorded.

CHAPTER 1

Background of Doctrine & Covenants 76
"The Vision"

In February of 1832, when the vision of the kingdoms of glory was received, the Prophet and his family had no home of their own. Joseph Smith and Sidney Rigdon had returned the previous year from a trip to Missouri and were commanded by the Lord to "seek them a home . . . through prayer by the Spirit" (D&C 63:65). Shortly after receiving this commandment, Joseph, Emma, and their adopted twin babies were invited to live with the John Johnson family of Hiram, Ohio. Father Johnson provided a "translating" room in the upper story of his home where Joseph and Sidney worked on revising the King James Version of the Bible, restoring many of the "plain and precious truths" that had been lost from the scriptures (see 1 Nephi 13:26–40). Sixteen of the revelations which now make up the Doctrine and Covenants were received in this room. Joseph had been working on this project periodically since June 1830, when he and Emma were living in Harmony, Pennsylvania. In 1831, the Lord had commanded Joseph and Sidney to lay aside their work on the Old Testament and to begin translating the New Testament (see D&C 45:60–62). It was while they were engaged in this effort that Joseph and Sidney received the revelation now found in section 76.

During this translation process, other people were often present. Seeing Joseph translate was an enlightening experience: "There must have been frequent periods of discussion about various passages and ideas. . . . The translation was not a simple, mechanical recording of divine dictum, but rather a study-and-thought process accompanied and prompted by revelation from the Lord" (Matthews, *"A Plainer Translation,"* 39). On this particular day, February 16, 1832, there were about twelve brethren present in the translating room. Joseph dictated and Sidney Rigdon wrote every word of the chapter they were revising.[1] While working on the fifth chapter of John, Joseph began to ponder the meaning of the two resurrections mentioned in verse 29:

> Marvel not at this: for the hour is coming, in the which all that are in the graves shall hear his voice,
> And shall come forth; they that have done good, unto the resurrection of life; and they that have done evil, unto the resurrection of damnation (John 5:28–29).

The Prophet later expressed his thoughts as he had pondered these verses:

> From sundry revelations it was apparent that many important points touching the salvation of man, had been taken from the Bible, or lost before it was compiled. It appeared self evident from what truths were left, that if God rewarded every one according to the deeds done in the body the term "Heaven," as intended for the Saints' eternal home, must include more kingdoms than one *(History of the Church,* 1:245).

As Joseph and Sidney studied these verses, the Lord inspired them to change the wording of the twenty-ninth verse from "the resurrection of *life*" to "the resurrection of the *just*" and "the resurrection of *damnation*" to "the resurrection of the *unjust*" (John 5:28–29, italics added). In reference to this experience, Joseph declared, "Now this caused us to marvel for it was given unto us of the Spirit" (D&C 76:18). Suddenly the heavens opened, and both the Prophet and Sidney beheld the glorious vision. Their experience is recorded in section 76.

MOONS IDS BOOKSTORE
112 PRESTON VALLEY SC
DALLAS, TX 75230
972-934-9988
1415801710702390

C O P Y
10/31/2000 16:43
Sale:

Transaction #   12
Card Type :   VISA
Acc: 4160871000490252
Exp. Date :   0602
Entry: Manual
Sale: 13.61
Reference No.:   00000012
Auth.Code :   031622
Response   APPROVED

We, Joseph Smith, Jun., and Sidney Rigdon, being in the Spirit on the sixteenth day of February, in the year of our Lord one thousand eight hundred and thirty-two—

By the power of the Spirit our eyes were opened and our understandings were enlightened, so as to see and understand the things of God—

. . . And while we meditated upon these things [i.e., John 5:28–29], the Lord touched the eyes of our understandings and they were opened, and the glory of the Lord shone round about.

And we beheld the glory of the Son, on the right hand of the Father, and received of his fulness;

And saw the holy angels, and them who are sanctified before his throne, worshiping God, and the Lamb, who worship him forever and ever.

And now, after the many testimonies which have been given of him, this is the testimony, last of all, which we give of him: that he lives! For we saw him, even on the right hand of God; and we heard the voice bearing record that he is the Only Begotten of the Father (D&C 76:11–12, 19–23).

Years later, the Prophet observed: "Could you gaze into heaven *five minutes*, you would know more than you would by reading all that ever was written on the subject" (*History of the Church,* 6:50; italics added). Joseph and Sidney's view of heaven, lasting for at least an hour, certainly yielded a vast amount of knowledge.

On this day, the two men saw a series of six visions. During these visions, the Lord repeatedly commanded them to write down what they had seen (see D&C 76:28, 49, 80, 113). However, at one point during the manifestation, the Lord commanded them *not* to write what they had seen (see 76:115). The six visions consisted of the following:

1) The Savior on the right hand of the Father being worshiped by holy angels (76:20–24).

2) Lucifer rebelling against Christ and being thrust down from the presence of God (76:23–29).

3) The sons of perdition suffering and going away into a lake of fire and brimstone (76:30–49).

4) The inhabitants of the celestial kingdom (76:50–7, 92–96).

5) The inhabitants of the terrestrial kingdom (76:71–80, 91, 97).

6) The inhabitants of the telestial kingdom (76:81–90, 98–112).

Philo Dibble was one of the twelve people present during the manifestation. He reported that he and the other men in the room "saw the glory, and felt the power but did not see the vision" (*Juvenile Instructor*, 15 May 1892, 303). Brother Dibble related some of the fascinating details of this experience:

> Joseph would, at intervals, say: "What do I see?" as one might say while looking out the window and beholding what all in the room could not see. Then he would relate what he had seen or what he was looking at. Then Sidney replied, "I see the same." Presently Sidney would say, "What do I see?" and would repeat what he had seen or was seeing, and Joseph would reply, "I see the same." This manner of conversation was repeated at short intervals to the end of the vision, and during the whole time not a word was spoken by any other person. Not a sound nor motion was made by anyone but Joseph and Sidney, and it seemed to me that they never moved a joint or limb during the time I was there, which I think was over an hour, and to the end of the vision. Joseph sat firmly and calmly all the time in the midst of a magnificent glory, but Sidney sat limp and pale, apparently as limber as a rag, observing which Joseph remarked, smilingly, "Sidney is not used to it as I am." (*Juvenile Instructor*, ibid.).

On another occasion Brother Dibble elaborated on this contrast between Joseph and Sidney:

> Joseph wore black clothes but at this time seemed to be dressed in an element of glorious white, and his face shone as if it were transparent,[2] but I did not see the same glory attending Sidney. Joseph appeared as strong as a lion but Sidney seemed as weak as water, and Joseph noticing his condition smiled and said: "Brother Sidney is not as used to it as I am" (*Juvenile Instructor,* ibid.).

Despite Sidney's fatigue, he stayed up the entire night writing his account of the vision (Barrett, *Joseph Smith and the Restoration,* 204). The experience stayed with him throughout his life; he later referred to the Vision in a stirring testimony:

> If any man says it is not the work of God, I know he lies. . . .We know here is the Church of God, and I have authority before God for saying so. I have the testimony of Jesus, which is the spirit of prophecy. I have slept with it—I have walked with it. The idea has never been out of my heart for a moment, and I will reap the glory of it when I leave this world. I defy man and hell and devils to put it out of my heart. I defy all, and will triumph in spite of all of them. *I know God. I have gazed upon the glory of God, the throne, the visions, and glories of God, and the visions of eternity in the days gone by* (*History of the Church,* 6:290; italics added).

The revelation was unprecedented in its doctrinal significance to the Latter-day Saints. But there is scriptural evidence that other prophets may have seen the same vision and taught the same doctrines in earlier times. Joseph Smith indicated that both Jacob in the Old Testament and the apostle Paul in the New Testament had seen visions of the kingdoms of glory: "Paul ascended into the third heavens, and he could understand the three principal rounds of Jacob's ladder—the telestial, the terrestrial, and the celestial glories or kingdoms, where Paul saw and heard things which were not lawful for him to utter" (*Teachings of the Prophet Joseph Smith*, 304–05). Jacob's dream of the ladder is described in Genesis 28:12: "And he dreamed, and behold a ladder set up on the earth, and the top of it reached to heaven: and behold the angels of God ascending and descending on it." Paul's experience of ascending to the third heaven is recorded in 2 Corinthians 12:2. Paul wrote that "a man" was "caught up to the third heaven." Referring to this verse, the Prophet Joseph Smith said,

> But St. Paul informs us of three glories and three heavens. He knew a man that was caught up to the third heavens. Now, if the doctrine of the sectarian world, that there is but one heaven, is true, Paul, what do you tell that lie for, and say there are three? Jesus said unto His disciples, "In my Father's house are many mansions, if it were not so I would have told you. I go to prepare a place for you, and I will come and receive you to myself, that Where I am ye may be also" *(History of the Church,* 5:425–26).

The Prophet made it clear that he himself had the experience of being "the man" caught up to the third heaven: "I know a man that has been caught up to the third heavens, and can say, with Paul, that *we* have seen and heard things that are not lawful to utter" (*History of the Church*, 5:556; italics added). In the often-quoted fifteenth chapter of 1 Corinthians, the apostle Paul clearly teaches the doctrine of the three heavens: "there are also celestial bodies, and bodies terrestrial; but the glory of the celestial is one, and the glory of the terrestrial is another. There is one glory of the sun, and another glory of the moon, and another glory of the stars: for one star differeth from another star in glory" (1 Corinthians 15:40–41). In the following quote, John Taylor makes a connection between these Biblical revelations of the kingdoms of glory and Joseph Smith's poetic rendition of his revelation:

> Our poet seems to be perfectly at home among heavenly worlds, and converses about their proceedings with as much familiarity as one could do about his domestic economy. He unlocked great and important principles which were indeed made known to the ancients; but which have been hid for ages: and when we contemplate the things that are unfolded we shall be led to say with Paul, "great is the mystery of godliness" (*Times and Seasons,* February 1, 1843, p. 81).

In spite of the biblical evidence, these doctrines were not correctly understood by those in Joseph Smith's day.

> The Prophet did not formulate a theology by merely elaborating upon ideas proclaimed by other American religious leaders. . . . An intensive analysis of the Prophet's teachings regarding life beyond the grave indicates that Joseph Smith unfolded a more reasonable, just, and comprehensive description of the future destiny of man than were taught by any of his contemporaries . . . Many aspects of Joseph Smith's teachings on the gradations of heaven were *different* from the views popularized by the Shakers and a few other religious groups of nineteenth century America. *The Prophet broached a distinct nineteenth century concept when he said that all men, except the sons of perdition, would be assigned to one of three degrees of glory in heaven* (Backman, *American Religions and the Rise of Mormonism,* 342–43; italics added).

The Vision was a major break, not only from what other American Christian communities were preaching at the time, but also from what the Latter-day Saints had known about the premortal and postmortal existence. Whatever the Prophet might have known before receiving the vision, the shock with which some of the Saints received these truths clearly indicates that *they* had never heard of such concepts. Brigham Young said, "My traditions were such, that when the Vision came first to me, it was directly contrary and opposed to my former education. I said, Wait a little. I did not reject it; but I could not understand it" (*Journal of Discourses*, 6:281). He also reported that:

> When God revealed to Joseph Smith and Sidney Rigdon that there was a place prepared for all, according to the light they had received and their rejection of evil and practice of good, it was a great trial to many, and some apostatized because God was not going to send to everlasting punishment heathens and infants, but had a place of salvation, in due time, for all, and would bless the honest and virtuous and truthful, whether they ever belonged to any church or not (*Journal of Discourses*, 16:42).

Like the apostle Paul, who beheld truths in vision that were "not lawful for a man to utter" (1 Corinthians 12:4), the Prophet and Sidney also received more knowledge during the Vision than they were permitted to record (see 76:115). Orson Pratt said, "There were things which they beheld which they were strictly commanded not to write, as the world was not worthy to receive them. Neither was the Church, at that time, prepared to receive a full knowledge concerning these things" (*Journal of Discourses*, 20:70). Joseph made an intriguing statement on the same subject: "I could explain a hundredfold more than I ever have of the glories of the kingdoms manifested to me in the vision, were I permitted, and were the people prepared to receive it" (*History of the Church*, 5:402). It is likely that over the remaining twelve years of his life, as the Church matured, some of these further truths were revealed to the Saints. For example, eleven years later in section 131 of the Doctrine and Covenants under the heading "Instructions by Joseph Smith the Prophet," Joseph presented the doctrine of exaltation in the celestial kingdom:

> In the celestial glory there are three heavens or degrees;
> And in order to obtain the highest, a man must enter into this order of the priesthood [meaning the new and everlasting covenant of marriage];

And if he does not, he cannot obtain it.
He may enter into the other, but that is the end of
his kingdom, he cannot have an increase (D & C 131:1–4).

Some members may have had difficulty accepting the newly revealed truths, but the Prophet and many others certainly did not. In his history, Joseph recorded that:

> Nothing could be more pleasing to the Saints upon the order of the Kingdom of the Lord, than the light which burst upon the world through the foregoing vision. Every law, every commandment, every promise, every truth, and every point touching the destiny of man, from Genesis to Revelation, where the purity of the Scriptures remains unsullied by the folly of men, go to show the perfection of the theory [of different degrees of glory in the future life] and witnesses the fact that that document is a transcript from the records of the eternal world (*History of the Church*, 1:252–253).

Wilford Woodruff, a 26-year-old convert from Connecticut, read a copy of the revelation before he met the Prophet. This future president of the Church declared, "Before I saw Joseph I said I did not care how old he was, or how young he was; I did not care how he looked—whether his hair was long or short; the man that advanced that revelation was a prophet of God. I knew it for myself" (*Deseret Weekly News*, Vol. 43, No. 2, p. 321).

CHAPTER NOTES

1. This method of writing every word was used at the time the Vision was received. More efficient methods were adopted later. In describing these changes, Reed C. Durham in his doctoral dissertation on this subject notes:

> [The previous] method of dictating and writing the entire text proved time-consuming; and in one sense, some of the work was needless as many verses were not being corrected by Joseph Smith, but were being dictated and written nevertheless. It appears, therefore, that they decided on a simpler method of recording the revisions. Only the verses needing corrections were written on the manuscript pages, and the books, chapters, or verses which were unrevised would either be written in the manuscript with the word "correct" after them, or else they simply were not marked or listed at all on the manuscript pages. It further appears that as their work progressed, in order to conserve more time, only the parts of the verses which were to be corrected, such as a line, a phrase, or even a word in the verse, would be written in the manuscript.

> While his scribe wrote the corrections as dictated, Joseph Smith, with a lead pencil and sometimes with pen and ink, made some minor corrections in the Bible, such as adding a few words, underlining key words, or crossing out some words. . . . In addition to these Bible corrections, Joseph check marked, before and after every verse which he felt or desired a needed correction should be made, and then dictated that change to his scribe, who would so note it in the manuscript (Durham, "A History of Joseph Smith's Revision of the Bible," pp. 51–53).

2. N. B. Lundwall adds the following note:

> Mrs. Sarah N. Williams Reynolds, of Salt Lake City, dictated the following highly important statement to the Compiler of this book: "I was a close neighbor of Philo Dibble who visited me very often. He had been very familiar and intimately acquainted with the Prophet

Joseph Smith, and took great delight in rehearsing his wealth of information concerning this acquaintance. Brother Dibble stated to me that the Prophet Joseph told him in connection with the others who were present in Father Johnson's home at the time the Vision was given to the Prophet Joseph and Sidney Rigdon, that (the Prophet speaking): 'MY WHOLE BODY WAS FULL OF LIGHT AND I COULD SEE EVEN OUT AT THE ENDS OF MY FINGERS AND TOES'" (Lundwall, *The Vision or the Degrees of Glory,* p. 11).

CHAPTER 2

Background of the Poetic Rendition
"A Vision"

Shortly after New Year's Day 1843, the citizens of Nauvoo had great cause for celebration. Joseph Smith and the Saints had just received the news that charges against the Prophet, accusing him of being involved in an attempt on the life of former governor Lilburn W. Boggs of Missouri, had been dismissed. Wilford Woodruff recorded that a day of fasting, prayer, and thanksgiving was held in Nauvoo on January 17, to express gratitude for the Prophet's "release and delivery" (Journal, 17 January 1843). Several new songs were composed and performed to honor Joseph and celebrate the good news. A close friend and personal secretary to the Prophet, William Wines Phelps, expressed his joy by writing a poem to the Prophet:

FROM W. W. PHELPS TO JOSEPH SMITH:
THE PROPHET.

VADE MECUM, (TRANSLATED.) GO WITH ME

Go with me, will you go to the saints that have died,–
To the next, better world, where the righteous reside;
Where the angels and spirits in harmony be
In the joys of a vast paradise? Go with me.
Go with me where the truth and the virtues prevail;
Where the union is one, and the years never fail;
Not a heart can conceive, nor a nat'ral eye see

What the Lord has prepar'd for the just. Go with me.
Go with me where there is no destruction or war;
Neither tyrants, or sland'rers, or nations ajar;
Where the system is perfect, and happiness free,
And the life is eternal with God. Go with me.
Go with me, will you go to the mansions above,
Where the bliss, and the knowledge, the light, and the love,
And the glory of God do eternally be?—
Death, the wages of sin, is not there. Go with me.

Nauvoo, January, 1843.[1]

During the next month, Joseph composed a 312-line answer to Brother Phelps' poem. The 78-stanza poem entitled "The Answer: A Vision" was published one month later (February, 1843) in the *Times and Seasons*. This was an incredible accomplishment given that we have no evidence the Prophet had ever written any poetry before this time. Some may feel that "The Answer: A Vision" represents literary talents beyond Joseph Smith's capability. The same skepticism is also manifest regarding his "writing" the Book of Mormon and other scripture. Through the power of the Lord, the Prophet was able to accomplish remarkable literary feats beyond his natural abilities. It seems evident that he wrote the poem with divine aid.

While Joseph may have enlisted the assistance of a more experienced poet, possibly even W. W. Phelps, in composing "the Answer," it seems clear that the work is primarily his own. This is based on four facts:

1) The Prophet was careful to sign only those editorials in the *Times and Seasons* which he authored. A year earlier, when he became the editor of the *Times and Seasons,* he published this statement: "This paper commences my editorial career: I alone stand responsible for it, and shall do for all papers having my signature hencefor-

ward. . . . Joseph Smith" (*History of the Church*, 4:551). The February issue of the *Times and Seasons* printed the Phelps poem *Vade Mecum* dated January, 1843, and "The Answer: A Vision," which concluded with the name "Joseph Smith" and the date "February, 1843".

2) The scriptural version of the revelation uses the first person plural "we" (Joseph and Sidney). The poem is written in the first person singular "I," such as in stanza 11, where the author says, "I, Joseph the Prophet," and in stanza 13, where he says, "I bear record as all prophets have."

3) When John Taylor, the editor of the *Times and Seasons*, introduced and commented on the poem, he acknowledged Joseph Smith as its author. After praising the poem for a column and a half, he concluded, "Modern prophets can prophesy in poetry as well as ancient prophets" (*Times and Seasons*, 1 February 1843, 82).

4) For February 24, 1843, the *History of the Church* records: "In reply to W. W. Phelps's *Vade Mecum*, or 'Go with me,' of 20th of January last, I dictated an answer: [It consisted of the 'Revelation known as the Vision of the Three Glories,' Doctrine and Covenants, section lxxvi, made into verse.]" (*History of the Church*, 5:288; bracketed material was added to Joseph Smith's entry by B. H. Roberts, editor).

In light of the above, it seems reasonable to assume that Joseph Smith is the poem's principle author.

John Taylor, a gifted writer himself, commented on the fact that although the poem may not be considered great poetry by literary critics, its content puts it in a class by itself. Highlighting some of the magnificent doctrines presented in the poem, he wrote:

The following very curious poetic composition, is at once both novel and interesting; for while the common landmarks of modern poetry are entirely disregarded; there is something so dignified and exalted conveyed in the ideas of this production, that it cannot fail to strike the attention of every superficial observer.

Uncontrolled by the narrow limits of this earth, and raised above all sublunary objects, his mind soars aloft unto other kingdoms, unravels the secrets of eternity, and contemplates the organization of worlds, in other spheres: the destiny of the living, the dying, and the dead are developed; together with the laws that govern other worlds, and the state of their inhabitants; the "heavens of heavens," open before his gaze, and the celestial kingdom; the habitation of the great "I Am," with all its resplendent, brilliant, and dazzling glory, bursts upon his sight. The Celestial, the Terrestrial and the Telestial worlds, with all their magnificence and beauty are open to his view; whilst the various states of their respective inhabitants, are presented before his vision. The dark and gloomy abodes of the departed lost, are also unlocked, and their confusion, and misery developed (*Times and Seasons*, February 1, 1843, p. 81).

Although the "common landmarks of modern poetry" are not necessarily followed in the poem, Elder Taylor says that Joseph, inspired by the spirit, wrote above the rules of poetry as had ancient prophets:

Concerning the style of the poetry, there seems to be a native simplicity, a brilliance of thought, and an originality in the composition, that can only be equalled in the oracles of truth; and by those who profess the same spirit; and when the muse of those ancient poets was fired by the spirit of God, and they spake as they were moved by the Holy Ghost, there was a richness a dignity and a brilliancy of ideas; and an exuberance of thought that ran through all their productions, as in the fascinating beauties of poesy they rolled forth the words of eternal life, with all their richness, and dignity, and glory; while at the same time they paid little or no attention to the rules of poetic composition. Let the curtains of heaven be withdrawn, and the purposes and glories of the eternal world burst upon his view and the dry forms; and the simple jingling of poetry, alone, will be very dry and insipid to the enlarged and enlightened understanding of a man of God (*Ibid.*).

For reasons that are not entirely apparent, the poem was not widely known and used after the Saints migrated to Utah. Only during the last half of this century has it resurfaced, and not until now has it had a publication specifically dedicated to it.[3]

CHAPTER NOTES

1. Ironically, Phelps' joy may have been tempered by the prophetic tone of the poem which foreshadows Joseph's death the next year. After the martyrdom, Phelps expanded and rewrote "Go with Me." He changed the perspective from addressing Joseph Smith to Joseph Smith addressing the Saints from beyond the veil and titled it "A Voice from the Prophet: Come to Me" (Michael Hicks, "Joseph Smith, W. W. Phelps, and the Poetic Paraphrase of 'The Vision,'" *Journal of Mormon History,* Fall 1994, p. 80).

2. Michael Hicks makes a case for W. W. Phelps being the principle author ("Joseph Smith, W. W. Phelps, and the Poetic Paraphrase of 'The Vision,'" *Journal of Mormon History,* Fall 1994, pp. 63–84). Richard N. Holzapfel supports the authorship of Joseph Smith ("'Eternity Sketch'd in a Vision': The Poetic Version of Doctrine and Covenants 76," *The Heavens Are Open: The 1992 Sperry Symposium on the Doctrine and Covenants and Church History,* Salt Lake City: Deseret Book Company, 1993, pp. 141–162). William H. Brugger believes Joseph and W. W. Phelps collaborated on the poem and suggests that a wordprint might provide more conclusive data ("Section 76 as Literature in the Doctrine and Covenants," Ph. D. dissertation, Brigham Young University, 1993, p. 100).

3. Richard N. Holzapfel surveyed the publication and use of the poem in the twentieth century and makes the following observations:

> That the poem did not receive much attention during the last half of the nineteenth century and the first part of the twentieth century may be because the early printed sources of the poem were not easily accessible. When the *History of the Church* was published in 1909, the text of [the] poem was not included, a significant lapse in making the document available to a wider audience in the beginning of this century. It was not until N. B. Lundwall reprinted it in 1951 that the poem generally became available. Several important twentieth-century studies neglect the poem altogether. A few more recent works make slight reference to it. A final group reproduce the poem in its entirety as an addendum but do not specifically cite it in their commentary ("'Eternity Sketch'd in a Vision': The Poetic Version of Doctrine and Covenants 76," *The Heavens Are Open: The 1992 Sperry*

Symposium on the Doctrine and Covenants and Church History, Salt Lake City: Deseret Book Company, 1993, p. 152).

CHAPTER 3

Illuminations, Amplifications, and Insights
from the Poetic Rendition

Comparing the poetic rendition of the Vision with Doctrine and Covenants 76 yields some valuable insights into what the Prophet learned during the manifestation and what he and Sidney Rigdon intended to convey in their wording of the scriptural account. Where the poem seems to "add" to the scriptural account, some readers may feel there is a conflict between the two versions. Readers who feel that way should naturally give the scriptures precedence over the poem, but there do not seem to be any major conflicts between the texts. The differences lie mainly in perspective and emphasis.

Many of these differences can be attributed to the fact that during the eleven years between the manifestation in Hiram, Ohio, and the writing of the poem in Nauvoo, both the Prophet Joseph Smith and the Church had matured and developed in many ways. The Church was not yet two years old when the revelation was received; and neither the First Presidency nor the Quorum of the Twelve had been organized at that time. Only half of the revelations which would later make up the Doctrine and Covenants had been received, and the powerful descriptions of the pre-mortal life and celestial astronomy found in the book of Abraham were yet to be revealed. The Pentecostal outpouring that would precede the dedication of the Kirtland Temple—including the visitations of Moses, Elias, and Elijah and their restoration of sacred keys, and the appearance of the Lord Jesus

Christ himself to Joseph Smith and Sidney Rigdon—would not happen until four more years had passed (see D&C 110).

The following insights gleaned from the poetic version are not comprehensive, but will hopefully encourage the reader to make a detailed study of the parallel, line-by-line comparison of the poem and Doctrine and Covenants 76. Such a study will yield a greater appreciation of both renderings of the Vision. The scripture and the poem each have elements not found in the other. The poem adds much to the scripture and the scripture adds even more to the poem. Since the scripture is well-known, this study focuses on what the poem can add to our understanding of the scripture.

Throughout this chapter, section 76 is referred to by numbered verses (76:1–119); and the poem, by numbered stanzas (1–78). As the reader studies the poetic additions, he or she may wish to refer to chapter 4, where the differences can be easily seen. In both chapters, the scriptural text is italicized. When a word or phrase is unique to one of the two versions, it is set off in bold type.

Sample Enhancements of the Scripture Text Afforded by the Poem

1. How the Vision Was Received

The Prophet gives two small but interesting insights into the process of revelation experienced on this occasion. When the scripture says, *"By the power of the spirit our eyes were opened"* (76:12), the poem says, "The eyes of the **inner man** truly did see" (11). For the scriptural phrase, *"The Lord touched the eyes of our understandings"* (76:19), the poem substitutes, "The Lord touched the eyes of **my own intellect**" (15).

2. Christ the Savior of Other Worlds

The poetic version's most significant doctrinal contribution to our understanding of Doctrine and Covenants 76 deals with the atonement of Christ. Verses 22 through 24 of section 76 suggest the possibility that Christ is the Savior of all the other worlds in addition to our own. In the poetic version, this profound doctrine is unmistakably clear. Concerning verse 24, Elder Bruce R. McConkie wrote, "In addition to the plain meaning of this passage, we have an explanation of it given by the Prophet Joseph Smith. He paraphrased, in poetical rhyme, the entire record of the Vision" (*Mormon Doctrine*, p. 65). A comparison of the two versions is as follows:

DOCTRINE & COVENANTS 76	POETIC RENDITION
22. *And now, after the many testimonies which have been given of him,*	18. And now after **all of the proofs made** of him, **By witnesses truly, by whom he was known,**
this is the testimony, last of all, which we give of him: That he lives! 23. *For we saw him, even on the right hand of God;*	This is **mine**, last of all, that he lives; **yea he lives!** **And sits at** the right hand of God, **on his throne.**
and we heard the voice bearing record that he is the Only Begotten of the Father—	19. And **I** heard **a great** voice, bearing record **from heav'n,** He's the Saviour, and only begotten of **God—**
24. *That by him, and through him, and of him, the worlds are and were created,*	By him, **of him,** and through him, the worlds were **all made,** Even **all that career in the heavens so broad,** 20. **Whose** inhabitants **too,** from the first to the last, Are sav'd by the very same Saviour of ours;
and the inhabitants thereof are begotten sons and daughters unto God.	And, **of course,** are begotten God's daughters and sons, **By the very same truths, and the very same pow'rs.**

This doctrine is also taught in two other places in the poetic rendition. Where section 76 verse 1 says, *"Beside him there is no Savior,"* the poem makes it even stronger: "And besides him there n'er was a Saviour **of men**" (2). Later, instead of using the scriptural term *"only begotten son"* (76:13), the Prophet says, "Jesus the Maker and Savior of all" (12).

3. Christ and His Mission

The role of Jesus Christ as the Savior of humankind is the central message of both section 76 and the poetic rendition. In addition to the numerous restatements regarding the Savior that can be found in the poem, there are a few additional words of praise and illumination for which there is no antecedent in the scriptural text. The fourth stanza of the poem is a good example:

> **4. His throne is the heavens, his life time is all**
> **Of eternity now, and eternity then;**
> **His union is power, and none stays his hand,–**
> **The Alpha, Omega, for ever: Amen.**

Stanza 33 also uses beautiful language to teach that Christ came into the world "to lay down his life **for his friends and his foes**" and to "bear away sin **as a mission of love.**"

4. Two Kinds of Beings Worshipping Christ

Verse 21 in the scripture mentions Joseph and Sidney seeing *"holy angels, and them who are sanctified before his throne."* With only that statement to go by, the reader might conclude "holy angels" and "them who are sanctified" are the same group of beings. The poem changes it to "holy angels **and hosts**" (suggesting those assigned to this world), and in a separate line, it not only speaks of "sanctified **beings**," but identifies them as coming **"from worlds that have been"** (17).

5. Premortal Life

Before the Vision was received in February 1832, the doctrine of the premortal existence of man was not clearly understood or taught in the Church. Section 76 verses 25–38 give information concerning the premortal spirits who followed Satan, but nothing is said concerning the righteous spirits who followed the Savior until they are living on the earth where Satan *"maketh war with the Saints of God, and encompasseth them round about"* (76:29). Fifteen months after the Vision was recorded (May 1833), the Prophet received section 93 of the Doctrine and Covenants, where the doctrine of the premortality of the righteous is taught (93:23, 28, 29). The doctrine was further revealed in the book of Abraham, which was published just two months later (see Abraham 3:22–23). The poem makes two references to the premortal existence that are not found in the scriptural text. In stanza 7, reference is made to "the **council in Kolob**," implying that at least part of the premortal experience took place on that planet nearest to where God dwells (Abraham 3:3). In the very first stanza, the Prophet confirms both the premortal existence of humanity, and his own foreordination: "**But before I return to my former estate, I must fulfill the mission I had from the Lord**" (1).

6. Satan

Satan and his fall from heaven are alluded to in the Bible (see Isaiah 14:12 and Revelation 12:7–9), and the Pearl of Great Price gives additional information concerning his fall (see Moses 4:1–4 and Abraham 3:27–28). Section 76 provides even more knowledge including the fact that Satan was *"an angel of God, who was in authority in the presence of God "* (76:25). Stanza 21 adds the adjective "**great**" to the word "authority" and refers to Satan as "**an angel of light**," and stanza 22 refers to him as "**the son of Perdition**." The poem uses another phrase that goes even further, referring to Satan's status before the fall as a "**Godified state**" (21). When the poem was reprinted in the *Millennial Star,* six months after its debut in the *Times and Seasons,* the word "Godified" was modified to "glorified." Whether Joseph Smith or the editor of the *Millennial Star,* Thomas Ward, or someone else made the change is not known. The same stanza (21) says that when Satan "Rebell'd against Jesus" he "**sought for his power.**"

7. Sons of Perdition

It is likely that the Prophet Joseph Smith received more information concerning the sons of perdition than any mortal ever has. He gives many details about them in the poem that are not included in section 76. They are presented here chronologically, mostly without comment:

A. The sons of perdition are overcome "**by the devil in warfare and fight/In hell fire, and vengeance, the doom of the damn'd**" (24).

B. They are guilty of "**despising my name**" (25).

C. They are "**of the world, or of men most forlorn**" (26).

D. They are "**Doom'd** to suffer **his** wrath **in regions of woe/Through the terrific night** of eternity's **round**" (27). The *Millennial Star* publication renders "**terrific night**" as "**long night.**"

E. "**Mis'ry's their doom**" (28).

F. "**By [the] Gospel they cannot repentance renew**" (29).

G. They must go to a "**great** lake of fire, **which burneth** with brimstone, **yet never consumes**" (30).

H. They dwell there "**while eternity goes and eternity comes**" (30).

I. "These are they, who must groan through the great second death" (31).

J. All but the sons of perdition are "made partakers of grace, by the power of his word" (31).

K. "They're lost; ever lost,/And can never return to the presence of God" (35).

L. This is "the torment apostates receive" (37).

M. They are "those,/Who remain filthy still in their anguish and woe" (39).

8. The Mission and Destiny of the Earth

The poem includes at least four references to the future of the earth that are not found in the scriptural text. After the scripture records the Lord's promise to *"make known unto them the secrets of my will"* (76:10), Joseph identifies one of these secrets as "when earth is renew'd" (11). The poem explains the purpose of this renewal of the earth: The Lord will "Sanctify earth for a blessed repose" (33), and he will "purify [the] earth for the Sabbath of rest" (34). The earth will then be sanctified "by the agent of fire, as it was by the flood" (34). Stanza 48 refers to this purifying by fire as "earth's second birth."

9. Celestial Kingdom

In section 76 the celestial kingdom is described as *"Mount Zion, . . . the city of the living God, the heavenly place, the holiest of all"* (76:66). Two additional lines in the poem enhance the description of this highest glory: It will be a place "where the blessings and gifts of the spirit abound" (49) and will be "the home of the blessed, the fountain of love" (50). The poem adds that the names of this kingdom's inhabitants are kept in "the archives of heav'n" (51), and in stanza 52 the poet reminds us that their celestial bodies are "mentioned by Paul" (52).

10. Terrestrial Kingdom

Those beings in the terrestrial world *"who died without law"* (76:72) are identified in the poem as "**the heathen of ages that never had hope**" (54). Where the scripture refers to terrestrial beings *"who received not the testimony of Jesus in the flesh, but afterwards received it"* (76:74), the poem makes clear where they *were* when they received it: "when they heard it **in prison again**" (56). The scripture refers to the terrestrial kingdom as excelling the telestial in glory, power, might, and dominion (76:91), but the poem adds that it also excels in "**light . . . splendor, and knowledge, and wisdom, and joy . . . blessings, and graces**" (65).

11. Telestial Kingdom

Elaborating on the image both Paul and section 76 use in referring to the telestial kingdom, the Prophet describes it as a "**starry world**" (58). The fact that the Savior's mercy extends to all three kingdoms, even to the inhabitants of the lowest, is made clear: "**For the leaven must leaven *three* measures of meal,/And every knee bow that is subject to grace**" (58; italics added). The Prophet Joseph Smith continues to describe the kind of beings found in the telestial kingdom. He indicates that not only do they fail to receive the testimony of Jesus as stated in the scripture (76:82), but also they lack "**evidence . . . that he ever was**" (59). Also the Prophet uses the poem to refute a common misconception that the telestial kingdom is hell—a place of suffering and unhappiness. He dispels this notion by making three references to the fact that in spite of their low status in the kingdoms of glory, the inhabitants of the telestial realm will be happy:

1) "**The terrestrial sends them the Comforter, though;/And minist'ring angels to happify there**" (62);

2) "**The telestial glory, dominion and bliss,** (64); and

3) "**The telestial region is mingled in bliss**" (69).

A few stanzas later, the scripture says the inhabitants of this kingdom claim to be followers *"of Paul, and of Apollos, and of Cephas . . . some of Christ and some of John, and some of Moses, and some of Elias, and some Esaias, and some of Isaiah, and some of Enoch"* (76:99–100). To this list, the poem adds **"Peter. . . Luther and Calvin, and even the Pope"** (70). Some followers of those on both of the above lists may eventually receive the full gospel and the testimony of Jesus and inherit the celestial kingdom; others of these same followers may be among the *"honorable men of the earth, who were blinded by the craftiness of men"* (76:75), and inherit the terrestrial glory. Those referred to in the context of the telestial kingdom, claim to be followers of the men listed above, but in reality are **"hypocrites, liars, whoremongers, and thieves"** (60). Joseph Smith observes in the poem:

> **They never received the gospel of Christ,**
> **Nor the prophetic spirit that came from the Lord;**
> **Nor the covenant neither, which Jacob once had;**
> **They went their own way, and they have their reward**
> (71).

The next stanza ends with **"In darkness they worshipp'd; to darkness they go"** (72).

12. Joseph Smith's Description of the Three Kingdoms of Glory

Concerning all of the three kingdoms of glory, the Prophet's poem says they are **"great, greater, greatest . . . [as] stars, moon, and sun"** (63), and they **"all harmonize like the parts of a tune"** (68).

13. Baptism for the Dead

Interestingly, baptism for the dead, which had not yet been revealed when the Vision was received, is mentioned in the poem written eleven years later. The prophet merely states, **"And then were the living baptiz'd for their dead,/That they might be judg'd as if men in the flesh"** (55).

14. Rewards for Faithfulness

The Lord offers glorious promises to those "*who overcome by faith*" (76:53). Those blessings include being "*sealed by the Holy Spirit of promise*" (76:53), being part of "*the church of the Firstborn*" (76:54), being among those "*into whose hands the Father has given all things*" (76:55), being "*priests and kings*" (76:56), and finally receiving "*his fulness and glory*" (76:56). Both the poem and the scripture use the phrase "overcome by faith." The poem adds "**and their works**" (43). Joseph teaches that overcoming by faith means "**being tried in their lifetime, as purified gold**" (43). He further identifies those with the power to seal as "**men called of God as was Aaron of Old**" (43). Finally the poem teaches what it means to be one "**unto whose hands he committed all things**" (44), "**for they hold the keys of the kingdom of heaven**" (44).

15. Joseph Smith's Description of the Vision

The prophet gives this succinct description of the glorious panorama he witnessed: "**Eternity sketch'd in a vision from God,/Of what was, and now is, and yet is to be**" (11).

CHAPTER 4

Side by Side Comparison of Doctrine & Covenants 76 and Joseph Smith's Poem

This chapter presents the poem in its entirety placed alongside the corresponding scriptural text so that the two can be read and compared easily.

The scriptural text appears on the left page, and the poetic version on the right. Corresponding wording and concepts are found as nearly as possible across from each other. Words and ideas found in one version but not the other are in bold print. The reader should not take every change in the poem to be significant, because many of them may have been made just to preserve the meter and rhyme of the poem.

By studying both the poem and the scripture, the reader can greatly increase his or her understanding of, and appreciation for, this magnificent revelation the Prophet Joseph Smith called, the Vision. What a blessing it is to have them both!

(Note: The scriptural verse numbers [76:1–119] usually do not correspond to the poem's stanza numbers [1–78].)

DOCTRINE & COVENANTS 76
THE VISION

*1 Hear, O ye heavens, and give ear, O earth, and rejoice ye inhabitants **thereof**, for the Lord is God, and beside him there **is no** Savior.*

*2 Great is his wisdom, **marvelous** are his ways, **and** the extent of his doings none can **find out.**
3 His purposes fail not, **neither are there any who can stay his hand.**
4 From **eternity to eternity** he is the same, and his years never fail.*

*5 For thus saith the Lord–I, **the Lord**, am merciful **and** gracious unto those **who** fear me, **and** delight to honor **those who** serve me in righteousness **and in truth unto** the end.
6 Great **shall be** their reward and eternal **shall be** their glory.
7 **And** to them will I reveal all mysteries, **yea, all** the hidden mysteries **of** my kingdom from **days of***

JOSEPH SMITH'S POEM
"THE ANSWER: A VISION"

THE ANSWER. TO W. W. PHELPS, ESQ.
A Vision.

1. I will go, I will go, to the home of the Saints,
Where the virtue's the value, and life the reward;
But before I return to my former estate
I must fulfil the mission I had from the Lord.

2. **Wherefore,** hear, O ye heavens, and give ear O ye earth;
And rejoice ye inhabitants **truly again;**
For the Lord **he** is God, **and his life never ends,**
And besides him there **ne'er was a** Saviour **of men.**

3. His ways are **a wonder;** his wisdom is great;
The extent of his doings, **there's** none can **unveil;**
His purposes fail not; from **age unto age**
He **still** is the same, and his years never fail.

4. **His throne is the heavens, his life time is all**
Of eternity now, and eternity then;
His union is power, and none stays his hand,—

The Alpha, Omega, for ever: Amen.

5. For thus saith the Lord, **in the spirit of truth,**
I am merciful, gracious, **and good** unto those
That fear me, **and live for the life that's to come;**
My delight **is** to honor **the saints with repose;**

6. **That** serve me in righteousness **true to** the end;
Eternal's their glory, and great their reward;
I'll **surely** reveal all **my** myst'ries to them,—
Tho **great** hidden myst'ries **in** my kingdom **stor'd—**

*old, and for ages to come, will I **make known** unto them **the good** pleasure of my will **concerning all things pertaining to my** kingdom.*

*8 **Yea, even the** wonders of eternity shall they know, **and** things to come will I show them, **even the** things of **many** generations.*

*9 **And** their wisdom shall be great, and their understanding **reach** to **heaven;** and before them the wisdom of **the** wise shall **perish,** and the understanding of **the** prudent **shall come to naught.***

*10 For **by** my Spirit will **I enlighten them,** and **by my power will** I make known **unto them** the secrets of my will—**yea, even those** things which eye **has** not seen, nor ear heard, nor **yet entered into** the heart of man.*

*11 **We, Joseph Smith, Jun., and Sidney Rigdon, being in the** Spirit **on the sixteenth day of February, in the year of our Lord** one thousand eight hundred and thirty-two—*
*12 **By the power of the Spirit** our eyes **were opened and our** understandings were enlightened, so as to see **and understand** the things of God—*

*13 **Even** those things which **were from the beginning** before the world was, which **were** ordained of the Father, through his Only Begotten Son, **who was in the bosom of the Father, even from the** beginning;*

*14 Of whom **we** bear record; and the record **which we** bear is the fulness of the gospel of Jesus Christ, **who is the Son, whom we saw and** with whom **we** conversed in the heavenly vision.*

7. From **the council in Kolob, to time on the earth.**
And for ages to come unto them I will **show**
My pleasure & will, what my kingdom **will do:**
Eternity's wonders they truly shall know.

8. **Great** things **of the future** I'll show **unto** them,
Yea, things of **the vast** generations **to rise;**
for their wisdom **and glory** shall be **very** great,
And their **pure** understanding **extend to the skies:**
9. And before them the wisdom of wise **men** shall **cease,**
And the **nice** understanding of prudent **ones fail!**
For **the light of** my spirit shall **light mine elect,**
And the truth is so mighty 't **will ever prevail.**
10. And the secrets **and plans** of my will I'll **reveal;**
The sanctified pleasures when earth is renew'd,
What the eye **hath** not seen, nor **the** earth **hath yet** heard;
Nor the heart of **the natural** man **ever hath view'd.**

11. I, Joseph, **the prophet,** in spirit **beheld,**
And the eyes **of the inner man truly did** see
Eternity sketch'd in a vision **from** God,
Of what was, and now is, **and yet is to be.**

12. Those things which the Father ordained of **old,**
Before the world was, **or a system had run,—**
Through **Jesus the Maker and Savior of all;**
The only begotten, (**Messiah**) his son.

13. Of whom **I** bear record, **as all prophets have,**
And the record I bear is the fulness,—**yea even**
The truth of the gospel of Jesus—**the** Christ,
With whom I convers'd, in the vision **of** heav'n.

15 For while we were doing the work of translation, which the Lord had appointed unto us, we came to the twenty-ninth verse of the fifth chapter of John,

which was given unto us as follows—

16 Speaking of the resurrection of the dead, concerning those who shall hear the voice of the Son of Man:
17 And shall come forth; they who have done good, in the resurrection of the just; and they who have done evil, in the resurrection of the unjust.

18 Now this caused us to marvel, for it was given unto us of the Spirit. 19 And while we meditated upon these things, the Lord touched the eyes of our understandings and they were opened, and the glory of the Lord shone round about.

20 And we beheld the glory of the Son, on the right hand of the Father, and received of his fulness;

21 And saw the holy angels, and them who are sanctified before his throne, worshiping God, and the Lamb, who worship him forever and ever.

22 And now, after the many testimonies which have been given of him, this is the testimony, last of all, which we give of him: That he lives!
23 For we saw him, even on the right hand of God; and we heard the voice bearing record that he is the Only Begotten of the Father—

14. For while in the act of translating his word,
Which the Lord in his grace had appointed to me,
I came to the gospel recorded by John,
Chapter fifth and the twenty ninth verse,
which you'll see.
Which was given as follows:

"Speaking of the resurrection of the dead,—
"Concerning those who shall hear the voice of
"the son of man—
"And shall come forth:—
"They who have done good in the resurrection of the just.
"And they who have done evil in the resurrection of the unjust."

15. I marvel'd at these resurrections, indeed!
For it came unto me by the spirit direct:—
And while I did meditate what it all meant,
The Lord touch'd the eyes of my own intellect:–

16. Hosanna forever! they open'd anon,
And the glory of God shone around where I was;
And there was the Son, at the Father's right hand,
In a fulness of glory, and holy applause.

17. I beheld round the throne, holy angels and hosts,
And sanctified beings from worlds that have been,
In holiness worshiping God and the Lamb,
Forever and ever, amen and amen!

18. And now after all of the proofs made of him,
By witnesses truly, by whom he was known,
This is mine, last of all, that he lives; yea he lives!
And sits at the right hand of God, on his throne.
19. And I heard a great voice, bearing record from heav'n,
He's the Saviour, and only begotten of God—

*24 **That** by him, and through him, and of him, the worlds **are and** were **created, and the** inhabitants **thereof** are begotten sons and daughters **unto** God.*

*25 And **this we** saw **also,** and bear record, **that** an angel **of God who was** in authority **in the presence of God, who** rebelled against **the Only Begotten Son whom the Father loved and who was in the bosom of the Father,** was thrust down from **the presence of God and the Son,***
*26 And **was called** Perdition, **for** the heavens wept **over him—he was** Lucifer, a son of the morning.*
*27 **And we beheld, and lo, he** is fallen! is fallen, **even a** son **of the** morning!*

*28 And while **we were** yet in the Spirit, the **Lord** commanded **us that we should** write the vision; for **we beheld** Satan, **that** old serpent, **even the devil, who** rebelled **against God, and sought to take the kingdom of our God and his Christ—***
*29 **Wherefore, he maketh** war **with** the saints **of God,** and encompasseth **them** round about.*

*30 And **we saw a vision of** the sufferings of those **with whom he** made war and overcame, for **thus** came the voice of the Lord **unto us:***

*31 Thus saith the Lord concerning all those who know my power, and **have been made** partakers **thereof,** and suffered themselves **through** the power of **the devil to** be overcome, **and to** deny the truth and defy my power—*
*32 They are they **who are** the sons of perdition, of whom I say **that it had been** better for them never **to have been** born;*

By him, **of him,** and through him, the worlds were **all made,**
Even all that career in the heavens so broad,
20. **Whose** inhabitants, **too, from the first to the last,**
Are sav'd **by the very same Saviour of ours;**
And, **of course,** are begotten God's daughters and sons,
By the very same truths, and the very same pow'rs.

21. And I saw and bear record **of warfare in heav'n;**
For an angel of **light, in** authority **great,**
Rebell'd against **Jesus, and sought for his pow'r,**
But was thrust down **to woe** from **his Godified state.**

22. And the heavens **all** wept, **and the tears drop'd like dew,**
That Lucifer, son of the morning **had fell!**
Yea, is fallen! is fall'n, **and become, Oh, alas!**
The son of Perdition; **the devil of hell!**

23. And while **I was** yet in the spirit **of truth,**
The commandment **was:** write ye the vision **all out;**
For Satan, old serpent, **the devil's for** war,—
And **yet will** encompass the saints round about.
24. And I saw, too, the suff'ring and **mis'ry** of those,
(Overcome **by the devil, in warfare and fight,)**
In hell fire, and vengeance, the doom of the damn'd;
For the Lord **said, the vision is further: so write.**

25. **For** thus saith the Lord, **now** concerning all those
Who know of my power and partake **of the same;**
And suffer themselves, **that they** be overcome
By the power of **Satan; despising my name:**—
26. Defying my power, and denying the truth;—
They are **they–of the world, or of men, most forlorn,**
The Sons of Perdition, of whom, ah! I say,
'T were **better** for them **had they** never been born!

33 *For they are vessels of wrath,* **doomed** *to suffer* **the** *wrath* **of** *God, with the devil and his angels* **in** *eternity;*

34 **Concerning** *whom* **I have** *said* **there is** *no forgiveness in this world nor in the world to come—*
35 *Having denied the* **Holy** *Spirit after having received it, and* **having** *denied the Only Begotten Son* **of the Father,** **having** *crucified him unto themselves and put him to an open shame.*

36 **These** *are they who* **shall** *go* **away** *into the lake of fire and brimstone, with the devil* **and** *his angels—*

37 **And the only ones on whom** *the second death* **shall have any** *power;*
38 **Yea, verily, the only ones who shall not be** *redeemed in the* **due** *time of the Lord,* **after the sufferings of his wrath.**
39 *For* **all** *the rest* **shall be brought forth by the resurrection of** *the dead, through the triumph* **and the glory** *of the* **Lamb, who** *was slain, who was in the bosom of the Father before the worlds were made.*
40 *And this is the gospel,* **the glad tidings,** *which the voice* **out of** *the heavens bore record* **unto us—**
41 *That he came* **into** *the world,* **even Jesus,** *to be* **crucified** *for the* **world,** *and to bear the sins* **of the world,** *and to sanctify* **the world, and to cleanse it** *from all* **unrighteousness;**

42 *That* **through him** *all* **might be** *saved* **whom** *the Father* **had** *put into his power and made by him;*

27. They're vessels of wrath, and dishonor to God,
Doom'd to suffer his wrath, in the regions of woe,
Through the terrific night of eternity's round,
With the devil and all of his angels below:

28. Of whom it is said, no forgiveness is giv'n,
In this world, alas! nor the world that's to come;
For they have denied the spirit of God.
After having receiv'd it: and mis'ry's their doom.
29. And denying the only begotten of God,—
And crucify him to themselves, as they do,
And openly put him to shame in their flesh,
By gospel they cannot repentance renew.

30. They are they, who must go to the great lake of fire,
Which burneth with brimstone, yet never consumes,
And dwell with the devil, and angels of his,
While eternity goes and eternity comes.

31. These are they, who must groan through the
great second death,
And are not redeemed in the time of the Lord;

While all the rest are, through the triumph of Christ,
Made partakers of grace, by the power of his word.
32. The myst'ry of Godliness truly is great;—
The past, and the present, and what is to be;
And this is the gospel—glad tidings to all,
Which the voice from the heavens bore record to me:
33. That he came to the world in the middle of time,
To lay down his life for his friends and his foes,
And bear away sin as a mission of love;
And sanctify earth for a blessed repose.

43 *Who glorifies the Father, and* saves all the works of his hands, except those sons of perdition *who deny the Son after the Father has revealed him.*

44 *Wherefore,* he saves all except *them—they shall go away into everlasting punishment, which is endless punishment, which is* eternal punishment,

to reign with the devil *and his angels* in eternity,

where *their* worm dieth not, and the fire is not quenched, *which is* their torment—

45 And the end *thereof, neither* the place *thereof, nor* their torment, *no man knows;*
46 *Neither* was *it* revealed, *neither is, neither* will be revealed unto man, *except* to them who are made partakers *thereof;*

47 *Nevertheless, I, the Lord,* show it by vision *unto many, but* straightway *shut it up again;*
48 *Wherefore, the end,* the width, *the height,* the depth, *and the* misery thereof, *they understand not, neither any man except* those

who are ordained unto this condemnation.
49 And *we heard* the voice, *saying:* Write the vision, for lo, this is the end of the *vision* of the sufferings of *the ungodly.*

50 And again *we bear record—for we saw and heard,* and this is the testimony of the gospel of Christ concerning *them who shall come forth* in the resurrection of *the just—*

34. 'Tis decreed, that he'll save all
                    the work of his hands,
And sanctify them by his own precious blood;
And purify earth for the Sabbath of rest,
By the agent of fire, as it was by the flood.

35. The Savior will save all his Father did give,
Even all that he gave in the regions abroad,
Save the Sons of Perdition: They're lost; ever lost,
And can never return to the presence of God.
36. They are they, who must reign with the devil in hell,
In eternity now, and eternity then,
Where the worm dieth not, and the fire is not quench'd;—
And the punishment still, is eternal. Amen.

37. And which is the torment apostates receive,
But the end, or the place where the torment** began,
Save to them who are made to partake of the same,
Was never, nor will be, revealed unto man.

38. Yet God shows by vision a glimpse of their fate,
And straightway he closes the scene that was shown:
So the width, or the depth, or the misery thereof,
Save to those that partake, is forever unknown.

39. And while I was pondering, the vision was closed;
And the voice said to me, write the vision: for lo!
'Tis the end of the scene of the sufferings of those,
Who remain filthy still in their anguish and woe.

40. And again I bear record of heavenly things,
Where virtue's the value, above all that's pric'd
Of the truth of the gospel concerning the just,
That rise in the first resurrection of Christ.

51 They are they who received the testimony of Jesus, and believed on his name and were baptized after the manner of his burial, being buried in the water in his name, and this according to the commandment which he has given—

52 That by keeping the commandments they might be washed and cleansed from all their sins, and receive the Holy Spirit by the laying on of the hands of him who is ordained and sealed unto this power;
53 And who overcome by faith, and are sealed by the Holy Spirit of promise, which the Father sheds forth upon all those who are just and true.

54 They are they who are the church of the Firstborn.
55 They are they into whose hands the Father has given all things—
56 They are they who are priests and kings, who have received of his fulness, and of his glory;
57 And are priests of the Most High, after the order of Melchizedek, which was after the order of Enoch, which was after the order of the Only Begotten Son.
58 Wherefore, as it is written, they are gods, even the sons of God—
59 Wherefore, all things are theirs, whether life or death, or things present, or things to come, all are theirs and they are Christ's, and Christ is God's.
60 And they shall overcome all things.

61 Wherefore, let no man glory in man, but rather let him glory in God, who shall subdue all enemies under his feet.

62 These shall dwell in the presence of God and his Christ forever and ever.

41. Who receiv'd and believ'd, **and repented likewise,**
And **then** were baptiz'd, **as a man always was,**
Who ask'd and receiv'd a remission of sin,
And honored the kingdom by keeping its laws.
42. Being buried in water, **as Jesus had been,**
And keeping the **whole of his holy** commands,
They received **the gift of** the spirit **of truth,**
by the **ordinance truly** of laying on hands.

43. **For these** overcome, by **their** faith **and their works,**
Being tried in their life time, as purified gold,
And seal'd by the spirit of promise, **to life,**
By men called of God, as was Aaron of old.

44. They are they, **of** the church **of** the firstborn **of God,—**
And **unto** whose hands he **committeth** all things;
For they hold the keys of the kingdom of heav'n,
And reign with the Savior, as priests, and **as** kings.

45. **They're** priests of the order of Melchisedek [sic.],
Like Jesus, (from whom is this highest reward,)
Receiving a fulness of glory and light;
As written: They're Gods; even sons of **the Lord.**
46. **So** all things are theirs; **yea, of** life, or **of** death;
Yea, whether things **now,** or to come, all are theirs,
And they are **the Savior's, and he is the Lord's,**
Having overcome all, **as** eternity's **heirs.**

47. **'Tis wisdom that** man **never** glory in man,
but give God the glory **for all that he hath;**
For the righteous will walk in the presence of God,
While the wicked are trod under foot **in** his **wrath.**
48. **Yea, the righteous** shall dwell in the presence of God,
And **of Jesus,** forever, **from earth's second birth—**
For when he comes **down** in the **splendor** of heav'n,
All these he'll bring with him, to reign on the earth.

63 These are they whom he shall bring with him, when he shall come in the clouds of heaven to reign on the earth over his people.
64 These are they who shall have part in the first resurrection.
65 These are they who shall come forth in the resurrection of the just.
66 These are they who are come unto Mount Zion, and unto the city of the living God, the heavenly place, the holiest of all.

67 These are they who have come to an innumerable company of angels, to the general assembly and church of Enoch, and of the Firstborn.

68 These are they whose names are written in heaven, where God and Christ are the judge of all.

69 These are they who are just men made perfect through Jesus the mediator of the new covenant, who wrought out this perfect atonement through the shedding of his own blood.

70 These are they whose bodies are celestial, whose glory is that of the sun, even the glory of God, the highest of all, whose glory the sun of the firmament is written of as being typical.

71 And again, we saw the terrestrial world, and behold and lo, these are they who are of the terrestrial, whose glory differs from that of the church of the Firstborn who have received the fulness of the Father, even as that of the moon differs from the sun in the firmament.

72 Behold, these are they who died without law;

49. These are they that arise in their bodies of flesh,
When the trump of the first resurrection shall sound;
These are they that come up to Mount Zion, in life,
Where the blessings and gifts of the spirit abound.

50. These are they that have come to the heavenly place;
To the numberless courses of angels above:
To the city God; e'en the holiest of all,
And the home of the blessed, the fountain of love:

51. To the church of old Enoch, and of the first born:
And gen'ral assembly of ancient renown'd.

Whose names are all kept in the archives of heav'n,
As chosen and faithful, and fit to be crown'd.

52. These are they that are perfect through Jesus' own blood,

Whose bodies celestial are mention'd by Paul,
Where the sun is the typical glory thereof,
And God, and his Christ, are the true judge of all.

53. Again I beheld the terrestrial world,
In the order and glory of Jesus, go on;
'Twas not as the church of the first born of God,
But shone in its place, as the moon to the sun.

54. Behold, these are they that have died without law;
The heathen of ages that never had hope,
And those of the region and shadow of death,
The spirits in prison, that light has brought up.

73 *And also they who are the* spirits of men kept *in prison,* **whom the Son visited, and** *preached the gospel* **unto** *them, that they might be judged* **according to** *men in the flesh;*

74 **Who** *received not the* **testimony of Jesus in the flesh,** *but after-*wards **received it.**
75 *These are they who are honorable men of the earth, who were blinded by the* **craftiness** *of men.*

76 **These are they who receive of his glory,** *but not of his fulness.*
77 **These** *are they* **who receive of** *the presence of* **the Son,** *but not of* **the fulness of the Father.**
78 **Wherefore, they are bodies terrestrial, and not bodies celes-tial, and differ in** *glory as the moon* **differs from the sun.**
79 **These are they who are** *not valiant* **in the testimony of Jesus; wherefore,** *they obtain not the crown* **over the kingdom** *of our* God.
80 **And now this is the end of the vision which we saw of the terrestrial, that the Lord commanded us to write while we were yet in the Spirit.**
81 **And** *again,* **we saw the glory of** *the telestial,* **which glory is that** *of the lesser,* **even** *as the glory of the stars differs* **from that of the glory of the moon in the firmament.**

82 *These are they who received not the gospel of Christ,* **neither the testimony of Jesus.**

83 *These are they* **who deny not the Holy** *Spirit.*
84 **These are they who** *are thrust down to hell.*
85 **These are they who shall not be redeemed from** *the devil until the last resurrection, until* **the**

Lord, even Christ the Lamb, *shall have finished* **his** *work.*

55. To spirits in prison the **Savior once** preach'd,
And **taught** them the gospel, **with powers afresh;**
And **then were the living baptiz'd for their dead,**
That they might be judg'd **as if** men in the flesh.

56. These are they **that** are hon'rable men of the earth;
Who were blinded **and dup'd** by the **cunning** of men:
They receiv'd not the **truth** of **the Savior at first;**
But **did, when they heard it in prison, again.**

57. Not valiant **for truth,** they obtain'd not the crown,
But are of **that** glory **that's typ'd by** the moon:
They are they, **that come into** the presence of Christ,
But not **to** the fulness of God, **on his throne.**

58. Again **I beheld** the telestial, **as third,**
The lesser, **or starry world,** next in its place.
For the leaven must leaven three measures of meal,
And every knee bow that is subject to grace.
59. These are they that receiv'd not the gospel of Christ,
Or evidence, either, that he ever was;
As the stars **are all diff'rent in glory and light.**
So differs the glory of **these by the laws.**
60. These are they **that** deny not the spirit **of God,**
But are thrust down to hell, **with** the devil, **for sins,**
As hypocrites, **liars, whoremongers, and thieves,**
And stay 'till the last resurrection **begins.**

61. 'Till the Lamb shall have finish'd **the** work **he begun;**
Shall have trodden the wine press, in fury alone,

86 *These are they* **who** *receive not* **of his fulness in the eternal world, but of the Holy Spirit through** *the ministration of the terrestrial;*

87 *And* **the terrestrial through the ministration of** *the celestial.*
88 *And* **also** *the telestial* **receive it** *of the administering* **of** *angels* **who are appointed** *to minister for them,* **or who are appointed to be** *ministering* **spirits for them; for they shall be heirs of salvation.**

89 *And thus* **we saw,** *in the heavenly vision, the glory* **of the telestial, which** *surpasses* **all** *understanding;*
90 **And no man knows it except him to whom God has revealed it.**

91 **And thus we saw the glory of** *the terrestrial which excels in* **all things the** *glory* **of** *the telestial,* **even in glory,** *and in* **power,** *and in might, and* **in** *dominion.*

92 **And thus we saw the glory of** *the celestial, which excels* **in all things**—*where God, even the Father, reigns* **upon his throne forever and ever;**

93 **Before whose** *throne* **all things bow in humble reverence, and** *give him glory* **forever and ever.**

And overcome all by the pow'r of his might:
He conquers to conquer, and save all his own.

62. These are they that receive not a fulness of light,
From Christ, in eternity's world, where they are,
The terrestrial sends them the Comforter, though;
And minist'ring angels, to happify there.

63. And so the telestial is minister'd to,
By ministers from the terrestrial one,
As terrestrial is, from the celestial throne;
And the great, greater, greatest, seem's stars, moon, and sun.

64. And thus I beheld, in the vision of heav'n,
The telestial glory, dominion and bliss,
Surpassing the great understanding of men,—
Unknown, save reveal'd, in a world vain as this.

65. And lo, I beheld the terrestrial, too,
Which excels the telestial in glory and light,
In splendor, and knowledge, and wisdom, and joy,
In blessings, and graces, dominion and might.

66. I beheld the celestial, in glory sublime;
Which is the most excellent kingdom that is,—
Where God, e'en the Father, in harmony reigns;
Almighty, supreme, and eternal, in bliss.

94 *They who dwell in his presence are the church of the Firstborn; and they see as they are seen, and know as they are known, having received of his fulness and of his grace;*
95 *And he makes them equal in power, and in might, and in dominion.*
96 *And the glory of the celestial is one, even as the glory of the sun is one.*
97 *And the glory of the terrestrial is one, even as the glory of the moon is one.*

98 *And the glory of the telestial is one, even as the glory of the stars is one; for as one star differs from another star in glory, even so differs one from another in glory in the telestial world;*

99 *For these are they who are of Paul, and of Apollos, and of Cephas.*
100 *These are they who say they are some of one and some of another—some of Christ and some of John, and some of Moses, and some of Elias, and some of Esaias, and some of Isaiah, and some of Enoch;*
101 *But received not the gospel, neither the testimony of Jesus, neither the prophets, neither the everlasting covenant.*

102 *Last of all, these all are they who will not be gathered with the saints, to be caught up unto the church of the Firstborn, and received into the cloud.*

103 *These are they who are liars, and sorcerers, and adulterers, and whoremongers, and whosoever loves and makes a lie.*
104 *These are they who suffer the wrath of God on earth.*

67. Where the church of the first born in union reside,
And they see as they're seen, and they know as they're known;
Being equal in power, dominion and might,
With a fulness of glory and grace, round his throne.

68. The glory celestial is one like the sun;
The glory terrestr'al is one like the moon;
The glory telestial is one like the stars,
And all harmonize like the parts of a tune.

69. As the stars are all different in lustre and size,
So the telestial region, is mingled in bliss;
From least unto greatest, and greatest to least,
The reward is exactly as promis'd in this.

70. These are they that came out for Apollos and Paul
for Cephas and Jesus, in all kinds of hope;
For Enoch and Moses, and Peter, and John;
For Luther and Calvin, and even the Pope.

71. For they never received the gospel of Christ,
Nor the prophetic spirit that came from the Lord;
Nor the covenant neither, which Jacob once had;
They went their own way, and they have their reward.

72. By the order of God, last of all, these are they,
That will not be gather'd with saints here below,
To be caught up to Jesus, and meet in the cloud:—
In darkness they worshipp'd; to darkness they go.

73. These are they that are sinful, the wicked at large,
That glutted their passion by meanness or worth;
All liars, adulterers, sorc'rers, and proud;
And suffer, as promis'd, God's wrath on the earth.

105 These are they who suffer the vengeance of eternal fire.
106 **These are they who are cast** *down* **to** *hell* **and suffer the wrath of Almighty God,** *until the fulness of times,* **when** *Christ shall have* **subdued** *all enemies* **under his feet,** *and* **shall have** *perfected his work;*
107 **When he shall deliver up the kingdom, and present it unto the Father,** *spotless, saying: I have overcome and have trodden the wine-press alone, even the wine-press of the fierceness of the wrath of Almighty God.*
108 **Then shall he be** *crowned with* **the** *crown of his glory,* **to sit** *on the throne* **of his power to reign forever and ever.*

109 **But behold, and lo, we saw the glory and the inhabitants** *of the telestial world,* **that they were as innumerable** *as the stars* **in** *the firmament of heaven, or as the sand* **upon the seashore;**
110 **And heard** *the voice of* **the Lord saying: These** *all shall bow the knee, and every tongue shall confess* **to him who sits upon the** *throne forever and ever;*

111 **For they** *shall be judged* **according to their** *works, and every* *man* **shall** *receive* **according to** *his* **own** *works, his* **own dominion,** *in the mansions* **which are** *prepared;*
112 And **they shall be** *servants* **of the Most High; but where God** *and Christ dwell they cannot come, worlds without end.*
113 **This is the end of the vision which we saw, which we were** *commanded to write while we were yet in the Spirit.*

114 But great **and marvelous** *are the works of the Lord,* **and the mysteries of his kingdom** *which he showed unto* **us,** *which surpass all* **understanding in glory,** *and in* **might,** *and in dominion;*
115 **Which he commanded us we should** *not* **write while we** *were yet in the Spirit,* **and are** *not lawful for man to utter;*
116 **Neither is** *man* **capable to make them known, for** *they are only* **to be** *seen and* **understood by the power of the Holy Spirit,**

74. These are they **that must** suffer the vengeance of hell,
'Till Christ shall have trodden all enemies down,
And perfected his work, **in** the fulness of times:
And is crown'd on his throne with his glorious crown.

75. **The vast multitude** of the telestial world—
As the stars of **the skies,** or the sands **of** the **sea;**—
The voice of **Jehovah echo'd far and wide,**
Ev'ry tongue shall confess, and **they** all bow the knee.

76. Ev'ry man shall be judg'd **by the** works **of his life,**
And receive **a reward** in the mansions prepar'd;
For his **judgments are just, and** his works **never** end,
As his prophets and servants **have always declar'd.**

77. But the great things of God, which he show'd unto **me,**
Unlawful to utter, **I dare** not **declare;**
They surpass all **the wisdom** and **greatness of** men,
And only are seen, **as has Paul, where they are.**

which God bestows on those who love him, and purify them-
selves before him;

117 To whom he grants this privilege of seeing and knowing for
themselves;

118 That through the power and manifestation of the Spirit,
while in the flesh, they may be able to bear his presence in the
world of glory.

119 And to God and the Lamb be glory, and honor, and
dominion forever and ever. Amen.

78. I will go, I will go, while the secret of life,
Is blooming in heaven, and blasting in hell;
Is leaving on earth, and a budding in space:—
I will go, I will go, with you, brother, farewell.

JOSEPH SMITH.
Nauvoo, Feb. 1843.

CONCLUSION

If this work has accomplished its purpose, the reader has come to appreciate Joseph Smith's poem as a wonderful and unique document that illuminates the great vision of the degrees of Glory. The poem does not in any way replace the scripture. But used properly, it can be a valuable aid in encouraging those who love the revealed word of God to learn more about the marvelous manifestation that the Prophet Joseph Smith described as "Eternity sketch'd in a vision from God" (stanza 11) and as "a transcript from the records of the eternal world" (*History of the Church,* 1:252).

As the reader studies the scriptural and poetic renditions of the Vision, may the Prophet's hope be more fully realized: "that every honest man is constrained to exclaim: '*It came from God*'" (*Ibid.*).

Joseph Smith—Prophet, Poet
Painting by William Whitaker

Sidney Rigdon—Joint witness of The Vision with the Prophet Joseph Smith

W. W. Phelps—Friend and secretary to Joseph Smith.
His poem prompted the Prophet to write the poetic version of The Vision.

WORKS CITED

Backman, Milton V. Jr. *American Religions and the Rise of Mormonism*. Salt Lake City: Deseret Book Company, 1965.

Brugger, William H. "Section 76 as Literature in the Doctrine and Covenants." Ph.D. dissertation. Provo, Utah: Brigham Young University, 1993.

Durham, Reed Connell, Jr. "A History of Joseph Smith's Revision of the Bible." Ph.D. dissertation. Provo, Utah: Brigham Young University, Provo, Utah, 1965.

Journal of Discourses. 26 vols. London: Latter-day Saints' Book Depot, 1854–1886.

Hicks, Michael. "Joseph Smith, W.W. Phelps, and the Poetic Paraphrase of 'The Vision,'" *Journal of Mormon History*, Fall 1994, pp. 63–84.

History of the Church of Jesus Christ of Latter-day Saints. Edited by B.H. Roberts. 7 vols. 2nd ed., Salt Lake City: The Church of Jesus Christ of Latter-day Saints, 1964.

Holzapfel, Richard Neitzel. "'Eternity Sketch'd in a Vision': The Poetic version of Doctrine and Covenants 76," *The Heavens are Open: The 1992 Sperry Symposium on the Doctrine and Covenants and Church History*. Salt Lake City: Deseret Book Company, 1993.

Journal of Wilford Woodruff, vol.2, 17 Jan. 1843. Historical Department. Salt Lake City: The Church of Jesus Christ of Latter-day Saints.

Juvenile Instructor, 15 May 1892, 303–304.

Lundwall, N.B. *The Vision, or The Degrees of Glory (Doc. And Cov. Section 76).* Salt Lake City: Bookcraft, 1950.

Matthews, Robert J. *"A Plainer Translation": Joseph Smith's Translation of the Bible, a History and Commentary.* Provo, Utah: Brigham Young University Press, 1995.

McConkie, Bruce R. *Mormon Doctrine.* 2nd edition. Salt Lake City: Bookcraft, 1992.

Phelps, W.W. "From W.W. Phelps to Joseph Smith: The Prophet," *Times and Seasons,* 1 Feb 1843, pp.81–82.

Smith, Joseph. "The Answer," *Times and Seasons,* 1 Feb. 1843, pp. 82–85.

Teaching of the Prophet Joseph Smith. Selected by Joseph Fielding Smith. Salt Lake City: Deseret Book Co., 1938.

Woodruff, Wilford. Sermon delivered at the Bear Lake Stake conference, August 10, 1891, *Deseret Weekly News,* p. 321.

ABOUT THE AUTHOR

Dr. Lawrence R. Flake is a professor of Church History and Doctrine at Brigham Young University. A thirty-eight-year veteran of Church Education, he has also served as president of the Missouri Independence Mission and as a Regional Representative of the Twelve. He is the author of a number of articles and numerous entries in *Encyclopedia of Mormonism* and *Encyclopedia of Latter-day Saint History*. His books include *Mighty Men of Zion, George Q. Cannon: His Missionary Years* and *Prophets and Apostles of the Last Dispensation*. Brother Flake and his wife, Elaine, are the parents of eight children.